THE STORY OF
THE WHEEL

TIM HEALEY

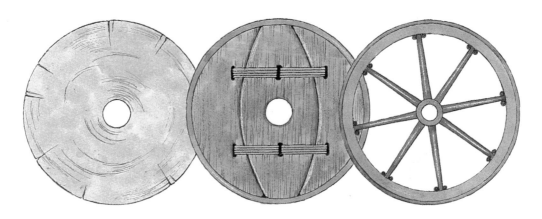

Illustrated by
NICHOLAS HEWETSON

Troll Associates

Library of Congress Cataloging-in-Publication Data

Healey, Tim.
   The story of the wheel / by Tim Healey; illustrated by Nicholas
Hewetson.
      p.   cm.
   Summary: Examines how the wheel has been used through history and
how it is being used today.
   ISBN 0-8167-2713-9 (lib. bdg.)   ISBN 0-8167-2714-7 (pbk.)
   1. Wheels—Juvenile literature.   [1. Wheels.]   I. Hewetson, N.
J., ill.   II. Title.
TJ181.5.H43   1993
620—dc20   91-40417

Published by Troll Associates

© 1994 Eagle Books

Design by James Marks
Edited by Kate Woodhouse

Printed in the U.S.A.

10 9 8 7 6 5 4 3 2 1

Contents

The first wheels

Nobody knows who first made a wheel. Long ago, prehistoric men and women simply dragged heavy objects along the ground or on heavy sleds. Then they discovered it was easier to move heavy weights if they were placed on rollers. They used logs for rollers. The ancient Britons, for example, probably moved huge stones on log rollers to make the famous monument at Stonehenge.

▼ Although it was a help to roll these great stones along logs, Stonehenge could not have been built without many people working very hard as well.

Later, someone had the clever idea of cutting slices from a log to make wheels. Two wheels could be joined together by an axle, made from a thinner log. This allowed people to make carts. The first carts had four solid wheels, two at the front and two at the back. They were invented in Asia about 5,000 years ago and were usually pulled by oxen.

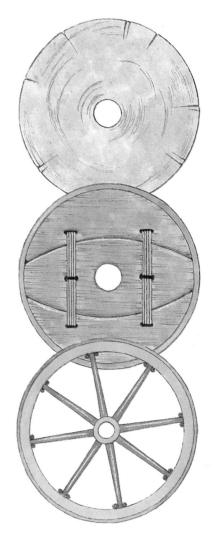

▲ These are three stages in the development of the wheel. First, a solid disk; second, three pieces of wood joined together for extra strength with an outer rim; and third, a lighter, spoked wheel.

5

Spoked wheels

The wheels of early carts were made from solid planks of wood. The planks were clamped together with wooden struts. These sturdy wheels were very useful for carrying heavy loads along rough roads.

But solid wheels were too heavy for speedy travel. Soldiers wanted vehicles that would go faster, and so wheels with spokes were invented. Spokes are rods that link the hub of a wheel with the rim.

▼ By 1600 B.C., the Egyptians were moving along faster than anyone had before that time in their light, two-wheeled chariots. They used their chariots successfully in battle, and for traveling around the country.

Spoked wheels were lighter and faster. At first these wheels had four spokes, but later they had more spokes and a narrower rim. The first horse-drawn war chariots were used by ancient people around 2000 B.C. The Hittites may have invented them in Asia Minor.

▲ This Sumerian war chariot had solid wheels and could not have moved very fast or been easy to steer.

Potters and pulleys

Wheeled carts made everyday life much easier. People could now bring huge quantities of grain and other food from farms to markets. Traders could move piles of goods from town to town. Networks of new roads were built to carry this traffic.

▼ The ancient Greeks were famous for their pottery. This father and son are working together making pots and vases, which they will then decorate.

But the wheel was not only used to transport things. Ancient potters used flat wheels, which they set spinning like turntables. These wheels made it much easier to shape and mold the clay when they were making rounded bowls, vases, and jugs.

▲ Ancient builders also used wheels. They cut a groove in a wheel fixed high above the ground to make a pulley. They fitted rope into the groove, and pulled on it to lift stones.

Windmills

Wheels were used in machines such as windmills. It was the wheel that made it possible to harness the power of the wind to grind grain.

The wind turned the great sails, and the sails turned gear wheels which turned the millstones. Gear wheels have cogs that fit into the cogs of other gear wheels. While the big sails turned slowly in the wind, the smaller wheels turned much faster. This made it easier to grind grain into flour for bread-making. Heavy, wheel-shaped millstones did the grinding.

The Persians made the first windmills in the 7th century, and windmills were being used in Europe by the end of the 12th century. Later, people used windmills to do other tasks, such as raising coal from mines and pumping water from wells. Today, windmills are sometimes used to make electricity.

◀ This simple windmill was built in open flat land, which was likely to be windy. Some windmills were built so that the sails could turn toward the wind.

▶ Sacks of grain were hoisted to the top of the mill. The grain was then poured down chutes to the middle level of the mill, where it was ground by the millstones. These were powered by a series of gear wheels leading from windmill sails. The ground grain was then poured into sacks as flour, ready for making bread.

Why no wheels?

Many people say that the wheel was the most important invention of all time. It is hard to imagine a world without wheels today. Yet the great civilizations of the ancient Americas had no wheels. The Incas of Peru and the Aztecs of Mexico had no wheeled carts, no potters' wheels, and no wheeled machinery. Why was this?

There are two likely reasons. First, there were no horses or oxen to pull the carts. Secondly, much of the country was dense forest, mountain, and swamp, which was unsuitable for wheeled traffic.

Nevertheless, the idea of the wheel was not unknown in the Americas. Some little models of wheeled clay animals have been found in Mexican tombs. So why did no one think of making large wheeled objects? The answer remains a mystery.

▲ Building pyramids with large blocks of stone was hard work without the help of wheels.

▶ The picture shows boys playing with wheeled clay animals. The animals date from the first century and were probably used as toys. Some people think, however, that their purpose may have been religious.

Clocks and watches

For hundreds of years people have been using wheels in clocks and watches. The first mechanical clocks worked by cords and weights. A weight was fixed to a cord wound around a rod. As the weight fell, the hands of the clock moved. The problem was to keep the hands moving at an even rate. A series of gear wheels helped with this. Such clocks were used in Europe in the Middle Ages, but they were big and clumsy.

Then, in the 15th century, someone invented the first clock to be driven by a spring. Instead of weights, a coiled spring provided the power to turn the hands. As the wound spring uncoiled, the hands turned. Again, gear wheels helped keep the machinery moving at an even rate. Clocks with springs could be made much smaller, and before long pocket watches and wrist watches appeared.

▶ This mechanical clock dates from the 16th century. The weights on the horizontal bars can be moved to regulate their swing. Because this clock was only accurate to the nearest hour, it was only necessary to have one hand.

The spinning wheel

The wheel made all sorts of jobs easier. One of the most important jobs was the ancient skill of making thread from wool. In early times, raw wool was spun on a revolving wooden rod, or spindle, that twisted the fibers into thread. A heavy disk was attached to the base of the spindle to help it turn. Then came the spinning wheel, which used a big wheel instead of a disk to help the spindle turn. Early spinning wheels were operated by hand, but foot pedals were added for faster action.

▲ Untangled cotton or wool was drawn onto the spindle, which spun the fibers until they became a smooth yarn. The yarn then slipped off the end of the spindle and was wound into a ball.

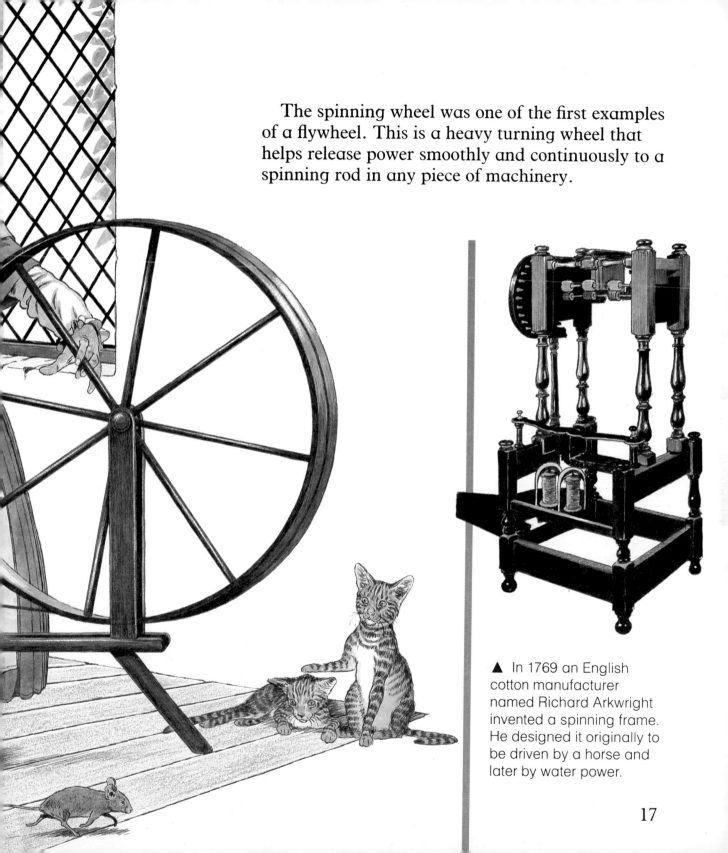

The spinning wheel was one of the first examples of a flywheel. This is a heavy turning wheel that helps release power smoothly and continuously to a spinning rod in any piece of machinery.

▲ In 1769 an English cotton manufacturer named Richard Arkwright invented a spinning frame. He designed it originally to be driven by a horse and later by water power.

Railroads

In medieval coal mines, the tunnels were steep and bumpy. To help coal cars travel more smoothly, miners had the idea of laying down wooden rails for wheels to run along. Later, horses pulled cars along the wooden rails. Iron rails came much later, and in 1806 a horse-drawn railway line for passengers was opened above ground.

▼ The present-day diesel train goes considerably faster than the "Rocket" of 1825, but both employ wheels running on a track.

At about the same time, the first steam locomotives were invented. A locomotive could pull much more than a horse. The first passenger-carrying railway in the world ran 27 miles (43 kilometers) from Stockton to Darlington in northern England. It was opened in 1825.

To keep a train wheel on its rail, a flange, or raised edge, was needed. Trains traveled faster and faster as the years passed. To help guide coaches and locomotives smoothly around curving track, the bogie was invented. This is an undercarriage with two, four, or six wheels. The bogie swivels as the train goes around a curve.

▲ This cross section of a wheel and rail shows how the flange keeps the wheel on the rail. Without it the train would slip off the rails.

The bicycle

In 1816 Karl von Drais invented a two-wheeled vehicle known as a draisienne. The rider sat astride it and scooted along by kicking the ground with his feet. Then, in 1839, a Scottish blacksmith named Kirkpatrick Macmillan added pedals linked by cranks to the back wheel. This was the first bicycle.

In the years that followed there were many different types of bicycles. One was the "ordinary" bicycle. It had a small back wheel and a huge front wheel. It was difficult to mount and riders often fell off.

The first modern bicycle was the "safety bicycle" of 1885. It had wheels of equal size, and the back wheel was driven by pedals and a chain. Riding became more comfortable after 1888, when John Dunlop invented air-filled rubber tires.

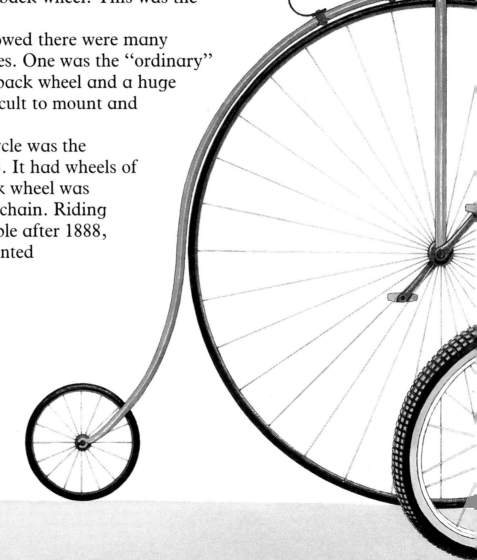

▶ The "ordinary" bicycle was sometimes called a "penny farthing." The big wheel was the penny and the small wheel the farthing, both coins in use at that time. Today's bicycles are much easier to ride. They come in all shapes and sizes, small enough for the youngest riders and fast enough for professional cyclists. Each of these types of bicycles has the wheels best suited to its use.

▲ Early bicycles had no gears. Some modern bicycles have about twenty gears. If you are going up a steep hill you can change gears so the wheels turn more often, which makes pedaling easier. The tires on modern bicycles vary. Racers have thin tires to be as light as possible.

Wheels in cars

The first motorcars appeared on the roads at about the same time as the first modern bicycles. The earliest gasoline-powered car was designed in 1885 in Germany by Karl Benz. It had two wheels in the back and one in the front. The front wheel was steered by a lever, which was not very safe. Since then, most cars have four wheels and are steered by a fifth—the steering wheel.

▶ A go-cart is like a simplified car. The wheels on these go-carts are very wide and thick like those of a racing car. They help to keep the cart steady and to lessen the likelihood of its overturning.

Rubber tires allow cars to travel at high speeds by reducing friction, the rubbing of the wheel's surface against the ground. Disk brakes were invented at the beginning of this century. This type of brake squeezes brake pads against both sides of a steel disk fitted to the wheel hub.

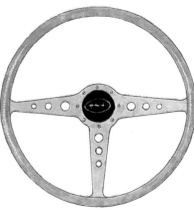

▲ The steering wheel in a car enables the driver to control the direction of the car accurately. The slightest movement triggers a reaction in a succession of gears which move the car's wheels.

Wheels of industry

Motorcars, bicycles, and locomotives all brought a great increase in the speed and amount of overland travel. Wheels also became important at sea, as massive engines turned the paddle wheels of steamships.

The period of the 18th and 19th centuries has been called the Industrial Revolution. Many goods were now made in factories, and machines did work that had previously been done by hand. Pulley wheels, gear wheels, and flywheels all played a great part in these changes.

Belted wheels also were important for transferring power from one revolving shaft to another. Examples of this are a fan belt in a car and a conveyor belt in a factory.

◀ This heavy machine moves along belted wheels which enable it to travel over uneven ground. They also help it to balance when it is pulling heavy loads.

▲ This series of wheels works like a conveyor belt. As each small cylinder turns, whatever is on it is moved along to the next one. It is a simple, but effective, method of moving things around.

Just for fun

Wheels have often been used for pure fun. Take the pinwheel, for example. This is a firework that spins in a circle around a pin, giving off sparks and colored flames.

The idea of "wheeled feet" goes back more than 200 years. The first roller skates were invented by a Belgian named Joseph Merlin in about 1760. He also made musical instruments. To show off his new roller skates, he went zooming into a ballroom at a London party, playing a violin as he went. Unfortunately, he could not stop, and crashed into a mirror!

Can you think of other ways in which wheels are used for fun?

▶ Skateboards are a recent invention. A skilled skateboarder can use the wheels to twist and turn in any direction.

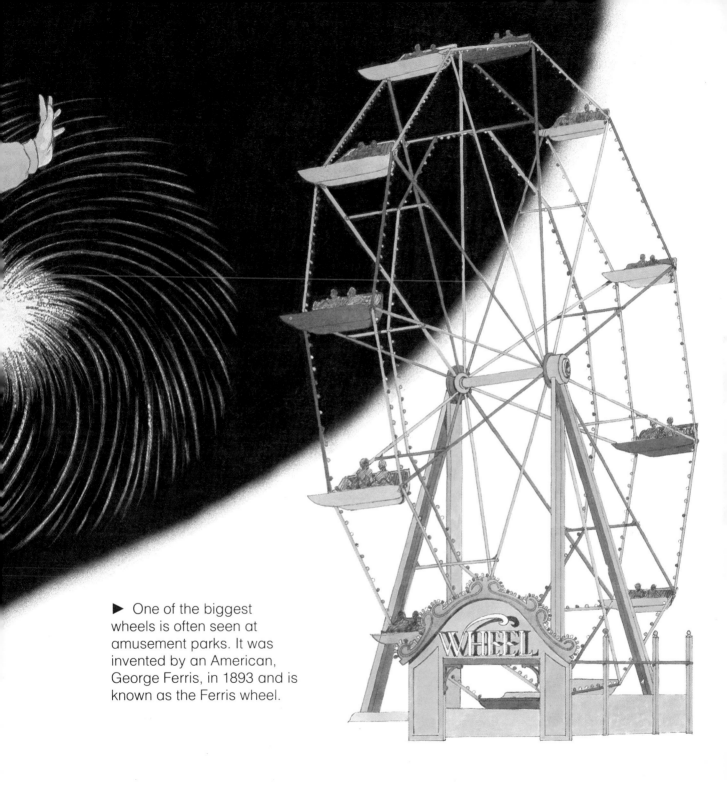

► One of the biggest wheels is often seen at amusement parks. It was invented by an American, George Ferris, in 1893 and is known as the Ferris wheel.

Flying wheels

Aircraft need wheels, too. An airplane is heavier than air and has to build up speed along the ground before it can take off. Wheels are also needed when a plane lands. The first manned flight in a powered aircraft was made by the Wright brothers in 1903. They were American bicycle makers, and so had plenty of experience in building lightweight, wheeled vehicles.

▼ This could be a space station of the future, an enclosed world spinning around the Earth.

▲ The tires of an airplane are very big. They must be thoroughly checked, as they have to bear a great deal of weight at a high speed. A punctured tire might cause an airplane to go off its runway.

Modern aircraft use a gyroscope. This important aid to navigation is a type of flywheel that acts as a compass. The gyroscope is kept constantly spinning, so that it remains stable no matter how fast an airplane changes speed or direction.

With all these uses over the centuries, it is easy to see why the wheel is said to be one of the greatest inventions ever made.

Fact file

Different wheels
There are many different types of wheels. A *cogwheel*, or gear, has teeth around the edge that link with the teeth in another wheel. A *flywheel* is a heavy wheel that spins in a machine to store energy and keep the machine running smoothly. A *pulley* is a wheel with a groove in it, used to pull or hoist weights.

Potter's wheel
Potters' wheels have been found in Mesopotamia dating back to around 3500 B.C. This may mean that the potter's wheel is older than the cart wheel. It is known that wheeled carts were in use in Mesopotamia by 3200 B.C.

Lighter wheels
Although wheels became lighter with the invention of spokes in about 2000 B.C., it was not until 1825 that wheels were used for a faster means of transport—the steam railroad. The first pedal cycle appeared in 1839 and the first three-wheel automobile in 1885.

How early wheels were made
We know how early wheels were made by studying vase paintings, scale models, and the remains of chariots found in royal tombs from 2500 B.C. In one example, a plank of wood was cut into three pieces of equal length. These three pieces were then joined to form a square. The square was then cut to make a circle, and finally a hole was made in the center

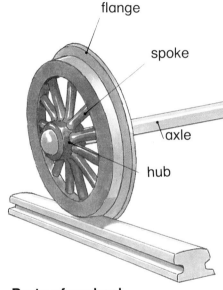

Parts of a wheel
Wheels can be disks, like a potter's wheel, or they can be more complicated, with different parts to them. The diagram shows the *axle* around which a wheel turns, and a *flange*, which is the protruding rim of a train wheel that holds it to a rail. It also shows the *hub*, which is the center of the wheel, and *spokes*, which run from the hub to the rim of the wheel.

for the axle. The wheels were bound with leather tires, kept in place by copper nails. The nails were not hammered right into the wood. They stuck out beyond the rim of the wheel and protected the leather from too much wear.

Bicycle wheels
Someone in Australia has built a rideable bicycle with wheels of only 0.76 inches (1.95 centimeters) in diameter. The largest bicycle wheel is "Frankencycle" with a diameter of 10 feet (3 meters).

Greater number of wheels
Although most cars have only four wheels, the longest car in the world has 26! Large trucks usually have double wheels as these are safer and can bear a greater load than one thicker wheel.

Waterwheel
This waterwheel is turned by the current of the river. As it goes around it takes up water, which then falls into a trough higher than the level of the river. The water in the trough (seen here in cross section) drains off to provide water for irrigation canals. This type of waterwheel was in use before 100 B.C. and is still used today.

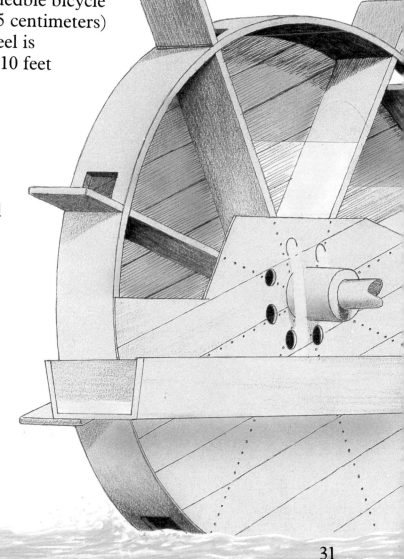

Index